ROLEPLAY

I0136497

ROLEPLAY

poems by

Juliana Gray

Dream Horse Press
California

Dream Horse Press
www.dreamhorsepress.com
Editor: J.P. Dancing Bear

Dream Horse Press
Post Office Box 2080
Aptos, California 95001-2080
U.S.A.

Gray, Juliana
     Roleplay
         p.100

         ISBN 978-1-9357161-6-7
         1. Poetry

10 9 8 7 6 5 4 3 2 1

First Edition

Cover: "Reel #4" by David Konigsberg
www.davidkonigsberg.us

for the staff, past and present,
of the sewanee writers' conference

Table of Contents

How dreary—to be—Somebody!
How public—like a Frog—
To tell one's name—the livelong June—
To an admiring Bog!

Emily Dickinson

In the end I was the mean girl
Or somebody's in-between girl
Now it's the devil I love
And it's as funny as real love

Neko Case

THE COSTUME PARTY

A Mad Hatter. A Star-Bellied Sneetch.
A couple of flappers—Zelda? Virginia Woolf?
My honors students, who've pillaged the thrift store racks
for literary costumes, shuck their coats
and tell me to guess who they're supposed to be.
Hester Prynne is easy. Quentin Compson's
suit is torn, and an iron hangs from his belt.

Then Kate, a girl I don't know well, clicks
into the room in black Mary Janes,
a pencil skirt, sweater—is this a costume?
Has she just come from work? I don't know what
to say except, "I like your stockings." She smirks.
I look again—isn't her blonde hair
a little darker? With newly sideswept bangs?
The stockings' teal pattern climbing her thigh?

Finally, I laugh. Of course, she's me,
or who she thinks I am—Dr. Gray,
with her long hair and sensibly sexy clothes;
Dr. Gray, who's fighting adulthood and age
by showing off her legs and partying
with undergrads; Dr. Gray, who
can take a joke. Kate and I laugh.
Tonight, she's me. And who am I supposed
to be? Somebody else, somebody else.

I.

Casting Call

PORTRAIT OF MY FATHER AS THE CORNER BAR

The hardwood floors have lost their shine, but gained

a certain honeyed softness born of use.

Sunlight bends through tinted windows veined

with lead. The wainscoting is coming loose.

The drafts, not unkind, are underscored

by whiskey, leather, sandalwood and mace,

as if a rakish vagabond had stored

his tired bags behind the fireplace.

There's always music, some discs overplayed—

DeBussy, Dylan, Davis, Dire Straits.

Each double-shining bottle is arrayed

for what it holds, or how it coruscates.

As for the regulars: a green-eyed cat,

two friends, at least one blonde worth looking at.

Portrait of My Mother as the Rush Hour Traffic Report

It's murder on the interstates tonight.
From high above in Action Chopper Nine,
the gridlocked lanes seem filled with firelight,
like torches of a mob waiting in line.
The highways aren't much better. Even routes
that only locals know—the two-lane street
behind the mall, the road that overshoots
your former high school—all ways spell defeat.
Why didn't you leave earlier? Why
didn't you plan ahead? We told you how
difficult it is, just getting by.
Action Chopper Nine can't help you now!
What's so great out there that you have to roam?
Be safe, be warm, don't suffer, stay home.

PORTRAIT OF MY SISTER AS A MARBLE ASHTRAY

Thick and darkly veined as river ice,
and yes, as cold, it rests its heavy base
upon the table edge, serving vice
without reproach, just silent, spartan grace.
In countless films noir and TV shows,
such simple bowls, taken up in passion,
have brained a hundred heiresses and foes.
This kind of death comes in and out of fashion,
but power always lies in its potential:
the sudden turn within the everyday.
It sits, meanwhile, seeming inconsequential,
taken all for granted: the passive ashtray
mutely serving the smokers without acclaim,
both holding and extinguishing the flame.

PORTRAIT OF MY EX AS THE LETTER X

At first you think it marks the spot: on texts

hand-inked on rolls of calfskin, mapping treks

to sites of opulent and tragic shipwrecks,

the legendary treasure of the Aztecs.

Then those same black lines shift in context.

A rating promises the kind of sex

they don't allow in the local multiplex.

In triplicate it flashes, calls and becks

to a lawyer with a desperate yen for latex

who, later, cleans his glasses and inspects

the document you've not signed, but hexed

with that same slashing mark, the intellect's

dilemma, the heart's unrelenting vortex,

the blank you'll never solve for: exactly X.

Portrait of My Cat as a Different Cat

She purrs with love and licks my face,

And always shits in the proper place.

SELF-PORTRAIT AS OLD BEDSHEETS

These linens purchased some vague years ago
would shame the mattress now. Folded, clean,
hauled to the garage, boxed and shelved below
the tools, the seeds, a can of gasoline.
Does this seem sad? A sentimental end?
When garden tomatoes bow in red defeat,
overburdened by their own fruit, rend
a pillowcase for ties. Use a sheet
for a dropcloth, or let the little neighbor boys
construct a clubhouse roof of cotton thread.
Cut whiteness into strips for darker joys:
wrists and ankles lashed to the poster bed.
Imagine these as comfort, brace, or noose.
They don't exist until they're put to use.

II.

Method

HELEN OF SPARTA

Twenty years and nothing's changed. The man
I married is still that man, though other husbands
and bedrooms overlooking richer shores
have come between that union and today.
Lacedaemon stinks of vinegar
and goats, as it always did. Menelaus
still picks his nose in court, still splits the bones
of pigs to scoop out marrow with his thumb,
still wipes his beard on skirts of serving girls.
Atop me in his bed, he calls me whore,
though that, too, is mere consistency.

The only thing that's changed is my own heart,
no longer a girl's, overripe with lust
for boys with lapis eyes and golden hair.
Now, I am a queen, obedient
and calm. When my husband entertains
our drunken guests with tales of his strumpet wife,
claims I bedded every prince of Troy
until old Priam, too, demanded a turn—
when my lord and husband says these things, I smile,
submit, retire to my quiet loom.
I do not drop a single linen stitch.

My jealous daughter, too, despises me.
Perhaps if I had borne a son. Perhaps
this one. Telemachus downstairs awaits

his gifts, silver cups and cloaks we'll send
to Ithaca. A poor substitute
for a father lost. I'll take the boy aside
and whisper that his father, like myself,
is merely delayed by pleasure and soft beds,
that lust is destined to subside. I'll sigh
into his ear, his golden hair that smells
familiar with oils. I'll breathe that man and wife
will be rejoined. Together they'll preside,
looking down from hard wooden chairs
side by side, as if nothing at all had changed.

Nancy Drew, 45, Posts on Match.com

Former girl detective seeks new mystery!
Looking for fun and possible LTR.

About myself: I'm single, twice-divorced
(long story short, the high school sweetheart
came out of the closet; the father surrogate
only wanted to bounce me on his knee).
I'm self-employed, still slim and titian-haired.
When I was young, I ran a little wild,
chasing after thrills and wicked men,
mad to drag the shadows into light.
Now I'm home, back in River Heights.
I'm tired of danger, of bombs and hot pursuits,
of being locked in closets, left for dead,
but I miss the rush—holding my breath in the dark,
listening for footsteps, feeling my heartbeat race.
Maybe—I hope—that's where you come in.

You: intrepid, fit, attractive (yes,
looks do matter!), bright but not a brain,
content to let the woman lead the way—
if life is like a dark and winding stair,
you follow as your lover carries the flashlight.

Turn-ons: lightning, crosswords, antique clocks,
secluded inns, pineapple daquiris,
pedicures, estate sales, roleplay, masks.

Turn-offs: liars, secrets, drugs/disease,
men with ponytails, the "b-word," guns.

Reply with recent pic. Kids OK.
My heart's a broken locket. Do you hold
the other half? Let's investigate.

FROM THE DIARY OF ADÈLE VARENS

Such strange events at Ferndean tonight! My mind
is all astir, my heart uneasy—yet I
will try to write without embellishment.

The day began fair; I passed the hours
in pleasant talk with Madame Rochester,
examining samples of fine lace and silk
for my trousseau; so playful was my joy
that I from time to time addressed my friend
as "Mdlle. Jeannette," a habit from the days
when she had been my governess; she smiled
whenever I would err. After tea
we walked among the woods and sunny fields,
remarking on the sapphire quality
of the sky, the summer blossoms, and Madame's
best-loved subject, how the grounds of Ferndean
compare to those of our former home, Thornfield,
lost these fifteen years ago to fire.
Madame remarked that though the Manor lacked
certain charms of Thornfield's grand estate,
she would not trade an inch of the humbler ground,
from which grew her present happiness,
for the stately stones of the past. "And look, Adèle—
see how the conkers from the great old tree,
the horse-chestnut struck by lightning at Thornfield,
have rooted in this shady earth, and grown
as tall as Mr. Rochester himself?"

But to the evening's strange events! We sat—
Madame, little Helen and her nurse,
myself—around the parlor fireplace.
Monsieur Rochester and his oldest son
had gone to Millcote to see to some details
regarding my upcoming nuptials,
which my guardian—who always had
seemed darkly stern, but whom, Madame assured,
had ever felt a quiet love for me—
had kindly offered to arrange. Monsieur
and Edward were not expected back until
the morrow, and so our party 'round the fire
was small but cheerful; when Mary entered the room
to tell Madame that there was come a gipsy,
an old and crippled beggar woman. She wished
to warm herself and eat a crust of bread,
and in exchange she swore that she would tell
the fortunes of any young ladies present.
How filled I was with curiosity!
Yet kept my silliness in check, eyes
lowered to my sewing. Still, Madame
did glance at me as she answered, "A gipsy, here?
Remarkable! And she has refused to leave,
I suppose, until she has discharged
this task? Very well then, Mary; show
her to the library." When she had gone,
Madame turned to me. "So still, Adèle?
I would have thought that you would be diverted.

But if you are not, or think this sybil a fraud,
as she almost certainly is, we can dismiss her."
My look must have betrayed my eagerness,
for she laughed, and nodded her consent.

The library was dark when Mary led
me there, promising to stay nearby
in case I should be frightened. The room was lit
by the amber glow of the hearth and a single candle,
beside which sat the gipsy, wrapped in layer
on layer of dusky cloaks, her hat pulled low
and held in place with a gaudy handkerchief;
one hand raised a pipe to her lips; the other
she kept tucked beneath her motley wrappings.
She did not look at me, but with the pipe
gestured at a seat before the candle.
"So," she said, her voice creaking like
a rusty garden gate, "you wish to have
your fortune told? Let me see your hand."
She clenched the pipe between her teeth and seized
my white hand within her claw; she bent
her head and seemed to study it, while I
did likewise. Even in the firelight,
the scars that marked her aged hand were clear.

"I see you are to be married soon," she croaked.
I gasped. "You see that written in my hand?"
"That, and more," she chuckled. "The gentleman

you wish to wed is a Frenchman, and a fool,
as are you." Snatching back my hand,
I said, "How dare you speak to me thus!
Monsieur Frédéric is not a fool;
his mother cared for me before I came
to England; they are a kind family,
and loved my mother." "But are you marrying
the family, or the man?" the crone rejoined.
At that I stiffly stood and turned to leave,
but she reached out her hand and clutched my shawl.

"I see you are offended; do not go.
I only meant that you are tender-hearted
and young; you do not know what marriage is.
Sit down again; I will not be so bold;
there, and listen. You are a pretty thing—
as fair and charming as your mother, though not
so vain, nor so coquettish—that too I saw
in your hand. You have had the benefit
of education, of loving guardians,
but you are ignorant of how a man—
or woman— may seem one thing, but reveal
another self entire. A gentle lady
may transform into a raving witch;
another maiden, seeming fairylike
and strange, may show herself to be the best
of earthly friends. Your Frenchman, then, I see
is kind to you, and dotes on you; but what

do you know of his heart? No need to speak—
I see it all—nothing, is the answer.
So little time have you spent in his company,
that you know nothing save his pleasant looks
and the love his mother bore for yours. Child,
I see you do not like this talk, so I'll
not keep you; but when you go and seek your friend,
the lady of this house, follow her
excellent example, and think! Not
on pretty dresses, nor the honeymoon,
nor even on your mother's memory;
but think upon your lifelong happiness,
and the man to whom you would entrust it. Now,
my child, you may go; ask the lady
if she would come and have her fortune told
as well; remember what I have said tonight."

The gipsy turned away and puffed her pipe;
I left the gloomy chamber and returned
to the parlor, where the brightness hurt my eyes.
Madame smiled solemnly. "Well, Adèle?
Did she tell your future, or your past?
Or does the ancient fraud only seek
to warm her bones?" I said that she could judge,
as the hag had asked for her. She smiled again,
strangely—how young she seemed, in that smile!
A long time she was gone, during which
I resumed my sewing and my chair,

but could not form a stitch. Likewise now,
writing in this diary, I find
I cannot make my thoughts conform to what
they ought to be. No doubt the crone is false,
or mad; her words shall not poison my heart
against Laurent, or the life we soon will share
in Paris. He is kind, and I do not doubt
my fondness for him will grow to love in time.
And yet how much the sybil seemed to know!—
how powerful the grip of that ravaged hand!—
how flushed Madame appeared when she returned
from her consultation with the oracle—
so much aglow, almost beautiful!

GHOST STORY

He had been gone for years, and yet he lingered—
or, since he had never lived in this house,
he just recurred— as she ate lunch, fingered
her graying hair, tossed a catnip mouse
to the cats. And there he was—no spook or shade,
not even a breath of wind, but still as real
as the gooseflesh on her arms. The ghost she'd laid
to rest in time had only been concealed.

What was haunted? A purple coffee mug.
Certain songs by Big Star. Summer cookouts.
Several DVDs. The bedroom rug.
Old jokes. Her hatred of Brussels sprouts.
How much of her reconstructed world was haunted?
Everything she lacked. All she wanted.

THE DEVIL PLANS HIS DAY

Up at daybreak with the crows. Starbucks.
Tell the anorexic goth barista
how beautiful she looks, and overtip.

Get the car hosed down by high school kids
and donate thirty bucks toward their trip,
by bus, to marching band nationals.

Pick up a hitchhiker. Tell her it's safe.
Deliver Meals-on-Wheels to widowers
and shut-ins. Hamburger steak, a little dry.

Meet a girl at the mall, talk a while.
She'll never have another kiss so warm,
so intimate. She'll always wonder why.

Coax a stray kitten to the porch
of a single mother and child, who'll fall in love,
love it like his own soul, until,

napping on the engine block, it's chewed
to bloody rags when Mommy starts her car.
The child will try to believe it's not her fault.

Judge a pile of poetry manuscripts;
award the prize to the emptiest, the most
abstract; to others, scratch a note: *So close!*

Early to bed with the snakes, pausing to give
thanks for this world of manifold delight,
for the blessing of such good work upon it.

Forest Creatures Prepare the Fairy Bride

Around her bodice, luna moths
did clasp their wings of green.
The ermine skirt hung restlessly
from the waist of tomorrow's queen.

Upon the backs of terrapins,
her feet appeared to float.
The bangle of a copperhead
coiled around her throat.

Ravens wove a trillium
into her hair of black.
A rawhide set with badgers' teeth
pulled her elbows back.

The spiders' dowry was a scarf,
invisible and fine,
they sealed across the lady's lips.
Oh, how her eyes did shine!

And last, the bridegroom fox did place
upon her hand the rings—
of glass? of gold? her mother's bones?
Heirlooms are such pretty things.

THE TIME MACHINE

"I'm damned if it isn't all going. This room and you and the atmosphere of every
day is too much for my memory. Did I ever make a Time Machine, or a model of a
Time Machine? Or is it all only a dream? They say life is a dream, a precious poor
dream at times—but I can't stand another that won't fit." – H.G. Wells

For reasons that have nothing to do with function,
he makes it beautiful: a glittering thing

of nickel, ivory, pearly quartz.
Golden bars curve out like sphinx's paws

or the slim runners of a Victorian sleigh;
the Deco wheel tilts like a parasol.

Will Neanderthals be impressed
by his burnished, scarlet, Spanish leather chair?

Will the children of a horrid future
coo and sigh, reward him with blossoms?

The Time Traveler is compelled
to see what man has done and made, will do,

what it will make of him, his fine machine.
He slips his arms into his smoking jacket.

Meanwhile, his body ticks its span of days
relentlessly forward, even as his mind

turns more and more toward its own past.
The Time Machine spins, grinding its gears.

THE SURVIVING TWIN

Even now, he cannot stop his eyes
from seeking, as a child does in the clouds,
his own face among indifferent crowds:
a mirror wearing nicer clothes, disguised
but nonetheless himself in suit and tie,
walking absently, his head bowed
until his brother waves and calls aloud
his name, he wakes, and grins in glad surprise.

No double self but one, he can't express
how each successive day without his brother
he's racked a little less by guilt and grief;
how, being just himself and not another,
he finds a pleasure in becoming less—
how vanishing brings something like relief.

Lyric I, Private Eye

Night in the city: the hour of cheap perfume.
I wandered lonely as a clod of mud
scraped from the worn-out sole of a salesman's shoe.
I shoulda been in bed, or knocking back
a scotch or three at Joe's; but I'm on a case.

I wander through the chainlinked streets, searching—
for what? It's complicated. A dame, sure,
who walks in beauty like the neon night
on legs like a ladder to heavenward.
A quiet bar where a guy can think in peace,
without these lights and sirens—either kind.
Plus, some stolen bird or diamond,
a purloined letter, an objective correlative.
My very soul? Hey, don't push it, pal.

They're after me, the hypocrite voyeurs
and thugs. They want to question me:
does nature restore my sense of self?
am I a persona? where'd I hide
the gun? does fog represent the sublime?
But I ain't gonna spill so easily,
not for those characters.
Those amateurs will never make me sing.

LOVE AMONG THE ZOMBIES

It's not the way you clean your rifle sight
with vinegar, or how you used your axe
the second day to hack a ragged skylight;

nor how you smile and let yourself relax
a little as you watch me honing knives.
When first we met, seeking the Adirondacks

and safety, fleeing the city for our lives,
I thought you were a jackass, the guy who takes
control of fuck-all, Lord of the Barely Survived.

Turns out Mister-I'm-In-Charge was Jake,
my husband. He hid the bite wound on his wrist
and called me a bitch before he died. At daybreak,

when he revived, I took the shot but missed.
I fired again, but didn't hit the brain—
he grabbed me, leaning in for a final kiss—

your hatchet gleamed, and blood like warm champagne
splashed across my face. You wiped my lips,
then helped me burn the body with propane.

Now, I watch the way you rock your hips
when you check the barricades. I always hold
the ladder so I can watch your ass, the rips

in your jeans, as you carry water down. This old
convenience store has medicine and food
enough to last us through the winter's cold.

Our booby traps and ghoul alarms are crude,
but loud enough to rouse us from the bed.
Let us love, enjoy our solitude,
let loose with screams and moans to wake the dead.

PHONE SEX

is not the subject of this poem.
I wrote that at the top so you
would start to read, thinking you
would be a little hurt at first,
but then get interested in what
I have to say about the Issues,
like Art and Love. Most likely Death.
I hope you don't feel tricked, but please
don't scan your eyes along these lines
in hopes that phone sex will recur.
Don't look for heavy breathing here.
Don't think about what the hand,
the other one that doesn't hold
the phone, is doing. There's just no way
I'm going to write about the voice
that whispers some scenario—
some fantasy about a hammock,
a girl with Angelina lips
and a pitcher of iced lemonade
from which she's just removed a cube
and drawn it slowly like a balm
into her ruby mouth as she
approaches you. Reader, put
that notion right out of your head.
Frankly, it's embarrassing.
I'm talking about Art, or Death,
so listen. I'll describe it. Stay
on the line. I'm almost there.

THE EVIDENCE

Now that the frozen ground is dusted white,
when each new morning shines with wan goodwill,
I see what the animals are up to at night.

Cats' paws criss-cross the porch's height.
Steam rises from a dog's yellow spill
below my sorry mailbox, dusted with white.

The heart-shaped prints of starving deer alight
wherever plants still show a greeny frill.
I see what these animals are up to at night:

They make my yard their own, leap and fight,
even underneath my windowsill.
I never knew, til the ground was dusted white.

The snow is glowing blue with flashing light
from a car at my neighbors' house, just down the hill.
What were those animals up to last night?

Official footprints lead within the site.
A gurney, heavy with a body— killed?—
writes its tale across the dust of white.
We see what animals get up to at night.

THE HOUSESITTER'S NOTE

Welcome home! I hope your trip was fun.
Around here, things were quiet. The plants
did very well, except the potted basil,
which wilted every day like it wanted to die.
I put it in the ground beside the porch.
Hope that's okay with you.

                              The cats and I
were instant friends. They'd curl up on my lap
or on my legs while I stretched out on your couch
and read your magazines. They slept with me
at night in your bed.

                         When I ran out of clothes,
I wanted to borrow some of yours, but they
were kind of snug. I lost eleven pounds,
eating only your salad, drinking your tea.
I chopped the toes out of your shoes.

                                        The mail
is on the table. I took the liberty
of writing to your teenaged son at camp.
His letters sounded lonely, and even though
he's far too shy, like you, to come right out
and say so, I think he had a wicked crush
on a counselor who's much too old for him.
I told him that we loved him, enclosed a ten.

When I got the midnight call that your dad had died,
I took the car, your good Kentucky bourbon
and drove out to the lake. I wept and drank
that warm bitterness, and when I smashed
the bottle on the rocks, the bits of glass
arced across the headlights' yellow beam
like far-off shooting stars.

                         Finally,
surrounded by the photographs of your friends
and loved ones, I softly passed away in your bed.
It's all right. It was my time to go.
And now, you'd never know that I was there
in your tidy house, your green and purring space,
except for a ghost of bourbon in the air
and, on your pillow, a single foreign strand.

THE BEARDED MAN

Sooner or later, a man will grow a beard.
It will not suit him, but he has his reasons.
Maturity is one, travel another.
In India, his razor will sit unused
in the pack he lugs to expensive restaurants
until he gives it to a beggar boy,
feels magnanimous, keeps the beard
as a souvenir. He'll have a child or two.
His father, whom he never loved, will die.

The beard will not look good—primitive
and scanty, gray and weirdly red. His wife
will search for gentle ways to let him know
it makes his face seem fat. She'll complain
it chafes her skin when they kiss. "It'll soften
as it fills out," he'll say, and kiss her less.
He'll trim it in the mirror, comb it, groom it,
think of Russian novelists. He'll love
the way it warms his cheeks, how he can keep
on skiing long after everyone else
retreats into the lodge. He'll volunteer
to take the kids Trick-or-Treating, dressed
as Paul Bunyan. He'll wonder secretly
if he can dye it white to play Santa.
Poseidon, Zeus. Some wrathful, vigorous god.

And then, one day, he'll see himself and flinch.
The magic will have fled; he'll see the fat,
the mange, the sad pretension. He'll move the book
of Tolstoy from his nightstand to the shelf.
In his wife's bathroom things, he'll find a pair
of tiny scissors. He'll snap a fresh blade
into the razor head, lock the door.
Each time he swipes the mirror fog, the face—
like those of passengers leaning out
the windows of a train nearing the station—
will clarify toward recognition.
He'll dab away the foam, clear the glass.
He'll tell himself he's a brand new man.

AUBADE

After making love, they lie entwined,
murmuring each other part by part:
her mouth, his collarbone, their hands aligned
fingertip to tip above his heart.
It's raining. His unit's shipping out tonight.
His body knows the length and shape of hers
like life, and holds it, pushing back his fright.
He wants to keep this moment, these sighs and stirs.
She thinks about the desert, if it's true
it never rains, just lonely wind and sand.
His waking light won't be this morning's blue.
A world she doesn't want to understand.
Every raindrop slams like a falling boot,
a roadside bomb, a funeral salute.

TWO SCENES

I.

Baby always liked it rough.
Tonight they'll play his favorite game.
Hogtie, ball gag, spreader, cuff:
Baby always liked it rough.
The joys in life are few enough;
why bore yourself? Why be so tame?
Baby always liked it rough.
Tonight they'll play his favorite game.

II.

She likes it that nobody knows
about the games they play at night:
the little pains, the quid pro quos.
She likes it that nobody knows
how caresses turn to blows,
how neckties bind her wrists too tight.
She's grateful that nobody knows
about the games they play at night.

ACTORS BETWEEN ROLES

Their sourceless words
hang like dead marionettes.

They seem to have forgotten
how to walk, how to use their hands.

Their well-lit mirrors
give back faces, faces, faces.

III.

Box Set

REAR WINDOW

Let us talk about voyeurs. Let's
admit that's what we are. Let us confess
that yes, we've glanced into those rooms whose glow
permits our stare while giving back mirrors
to those secure inside. And yes, we've placed
ourselves on blind display, chosen not
to pull the drapes, lived tableaux vivants:
a family at dinner, a woman reading,
a party, pantomime of clinking glass
and bared teeth that might as well be laughter.

It's summer. Everyone's drapes are opened wide
for the breeze, or hope of breeze. Like honeycombs,
the windows' golden cells emit the hum
of life. The songwriter pecks out notes
that spurn his advances toward a melody.
The ballerina flips her ponytail,
stirs her hips and a pitcher of strong martinis.
The salesman turns his silent back on his wife.
The spinster of thirty-five, Miss Lonelyhearts,
drinks a toast to an empty chair and sobs,
ruining the silk of her favorite dress.

Which of these do you prefer? Where
shall we turn our gaze, focus the lens?
Hypocrite voyeur—mon semblable—mon frère—
you may take your choice of miseries.

PSYCHO

It never fails: driving past
some lowland marsh thick with stumps
and sunning stinkpot turtles, I think,
a perfect place to dump the body.

Never mind whose body—I have
no candidates—or why. I've learned
the mantra, *location location location,*
the three rules of homicide.

Or is it point of view? Think
of the wordless scene when Norman Bates
has pushed the car into the swamp.
The girl inside the trunk has been
our heroine—we've followed her
through desperate love, theft and flight.

Slashed, naked, open-eyed,
wrapped in a cheap plastic curtain,
she's gone where we can't follow.
What can we do but cling to Norman?
With him we watch the car sink
into the bubbling black, and when
it stops—the trunk, reluctant, paused
above the marsh—what can we do
but whisper *sink, go down, down!*
And then it does. The nervous boy

lets go the breath he's held and chews
another piece of the candy corn
he keeps in his pocket. Like a child,
our Norman; so dutiful, so sweet.

SUSPICION

The glass of milk
$\qquad$ glows:
a spot of light
on the darkened stair,
like a small moon
on a silver tray.
The husband's face
$\qquad$ is shadowed
as he carries the milk,
white as arsenic,
taking each step
with such deliberate slowness,
he doesn't spill a luminous
$\qquad$ drop.

His wife upstairs
no longer knows
who she married.
Is he lazy, but honest?
Is he a murderer?
That glass of milk—
$\qquad$ it glows.

Twilight, the ambivalent hour
between day and night,
between dog and wolf.
Suspicion climbs the stairs.

She'll have to drink

To know whose teeth are kissing

her throat.

STRANGERS ON A TRAIN

Why was Hitch so hard on the homely girls?
So many mousy gals in cats-eye glasses
sighing over Cary or Jimmy while they
pursued the chaste Nordic goddesses—
so many brainy little sisters, squeaking
like neglected hinges—he set them up
to knock them down, and made it seem like fun.
His daughter Pat, in *Psycho*, acts the part
of office girl and straight man, supposing that
the heel who fanned Janet Leigh's breasts
with twenty grand didn't flirt with *her*
because "he must have noticed my wedding ring."
Is this comedy? Did she think so,
as she took direction from the bovine face
that so resembled hers?

               Here's Pat again
in *Strangers* as Barbara, the kid sister
in glasses, handmaiden to the goddess.
She also plays a ghost, the double for
Miriam, the murdered Plain Jane wife.
What Bruno sees reflected in her glasses,
her big cowlike eyes, is the girl he killed.
He sees her at the carnival, still married
to the tennis star, pregnant by
another man, escorted by two more
out to cop a feel in the Tunnel of Love.

She'll let them, gladly. She'd let Bruno, too,
and that's the thing he cannot stand, cannot
abide remembering—her gawky stares
attempting some seduction, the clumsy way
she wrapped her mouth around the ice cream cone,
the come-hither smile on the homely face
as he knocked the glasses off and strangled her.
As now he'd like to strangle Barbara.

That's some fun, Hitch. That's a father's love.

THE BIRDS

We talked about this movie, right?
When we were married? Movie quotes,
allusions to books and bad TV

were all we talked about, it seems,
in the last months. All right, years.
The stitches fastening our days.

I think we must have watched as Tippi
climbed the stairs, the house asleep
except for the fluttering overhead.

The birds were waiting. They knew she'd come.
And still you asked, "Why the hell
does she go up there? She knows what it is."

She pushes open the door, lifts
the lamp. As if Bluebeard's wives
had been transformed, they fly at her.

Pecking, pulling. The dime-sized wound
on her temple, darkly bleeding. I said
something about playing a role.

Later, washing dishes, turning
around the tiny renters' kitchen
and managing never to touch,

we must have talked about the ending:

the lines of gray, patient birds,

unmoving, unresolved.

FRENZY

This one is hard to watch. In England, freed
from censors, Hitchcock gives us something real.
A rape. He makes it ugly. Naked breasts,
made ugly, spilled from a torn blouse.
The body, splayed and strangled, on display.

In grade school, I had a friend—a stupid girl,
probably retarded, though people used
more gentle words like "slow"—whose body swells
I envied. She had breasts and pubic hair
at twelve. I was skinny and flat as the book
 I carried against my chest to hide the absence.

We grew apart, which is to say, I stopped
returning her calls. Then she moved away.
When we were twenty, she was kidnapped, raped,
and murdered. Hikers found her, naked and bound
with her own panty hose, in a ravine.
Lengths of hose were looped around her wrists
and neck, so struggling only choked herself.
I saw a drawing the killer made in jail.

Perhaps that's why we're granted a little grace.
In the second rape, the camera pulls away
from the killer's door, backs down the hall and stairs
like a frightened child, retreats to the public street,
its safety and anonymous noise. We see

the row of curtained windows, but do not know
which one we should avoid looking at.

I prefer to think of the memorial tree
her mother dedicated at her school.
On a pale, soft February morning,
running in solitude across the green
expanse of the strange campus, I glanced
at the plaque, stopped, and stood there, breathing steam.
It was a pecan, I think. Her name, her dates.
The leaves were just beginning to unfurl.

ROPE

Cut a Throat Week? Strangulation Day?
He isn't joking, but don't believe a word.
The master of misdirection, of slaughtered stars
and undercover blondes, has tricked us again:
he's made us think this film's about a murder.

Look closer. It's 1948,
and two young men in tasteful suits, who share
this vast, immaculate apartment, men
who bicker like old marrieds, are having a party.
Inside the chest, the body of their friend,
the party guest who isn't really missing.
Oh yes, there's been a murder—

                                        but what's inside
the chest is simpler, more damning: a secret.
They've shut their secret in a chest, but failed
to lock it. They've covered it with damask, lit
candles on it, served the dinner from it.
All the party guests are tainted with it.

And when their mentor reaches for the hasp,
they don't make a move to stop him. They wait,
almost eager, flushed and out of breath,
as he opens the lid, exposes the thing
that they so feared, so longed for him to see.

NORTH BY NORTHWEST

What is there to say about a cornfield?
What has it to do with mortal fear?
The family at the summer festival,
having stowed their u-pick blueberries
and peach preserves in their minivan,
decides to stroll into the A-Maize-ing Maze.
At first they stay together, but when the kids
run ahead, split off down the rows,
finally outrun their laughter's ring,
the parents are relieved. They admit it.
He takes her hand, a thing he never does
in public; she leans easily into him.
They're pushing forty; they met at Vanderbilt
in graduate school, submersed in irony
and feminist theory; they have never walked
like this before. He stretches his free hand
and taps the stalks—such a healthy green,
the essence of green—as if for luck as they pass.
She scans the sky, tells him she's looking out
for cropdusters. She remembers a story:
that Cary Grant, hunkered between the rows
as if the bladed leaves would shelter him
from the strafing fire, did not seem terrified
enough. So Hitchcock took his leading man
aside and said, "Somewhere in this field
I have placed a large tarantula."
That was all. There was no fear unknown

to him, and Grant delivered his performance.
The woman in the labyrinth recalls,
but does not tell, this story. She notices
the tassels, the shade of gold nearest the ears,
the very shade of their daughter's hair. She strokes
her thumb along her husband's hand as wind
disturbs the corn just enough to stir
the chattering stalks, their ripened, dying talk
that they prefer to keep among themselves.

VERTIGO

Softness, riding the cicada crest
of a Sunday afternoon, my father and I
each would choose a word: *Dragon. Fist.*
Revenge. Blood. Then open up the paper

to check our guess against the listed name
of TBS's kung fu matinee.
Experience almost guaranteed
that one or both of us would win the bet.

Then tall Cokes in tumblers cracking with ice,
a nuked bag of popcorn, a cozy spot
on the old beige and floral sectional,
and we'd settle in to watch those fists, that blood.

This was Alabama, and I was twelve,
eleven, working on my irony
the way some kids worked on algebra
or slow knuckleballs. My father worked

on me. Already I knew Dylan, Cash
and the Beatles, read some Hemingway, preferred
Fitzgerald and Steinbeck, could chop asparagus
and onions for his risotto, and stir the pan

while he refilled his glass of cabernet.
At school, the kids asked if I were saved
and mocked my penny loafers. At home with Dad,
I learned how tall girls ought to walk, head high.

And Hitchcock. One by one he rented them.
Sometimes Mom would join us, but always Dad
and I would watch as Cary or Jimmy won
the icy blonde, saved the day or themselves.

In *Vertigo*, Judy hates the way
Scotty turns her into Madeline.
She hates the auburn hair dyed platinum,
last year's suit he says looks well on her,

the elegant suit his dead lover wore.
She's playing the role, his Madeline reborn,
as she played the role before, the Madeline
he fell for and watched fall from the tower.

Why can't he love her for herself, for Judy?
She hates it, but she goes along, for love.
She wears the suit, plucks her brows, dyes
her hair and wears it in the spiral twist.

Being made with care means being loved.
My father gave me hazel eyes, the Stones,
Greek mythology, gumbo, Yeats,
and how to use two different types of corkscrew.

In the Spanish mission, bells, hold your tongues.
Let no inquiring nun push up the door.
No footfalls on the stairs. Let us stand
without falling, pointing into the view.

IV.

Against Type

"Winter comes to rule the varied year"

Gone, the ripe tomato. Gone, the tang,
almost of wine, at its greeny stem. Gone,
the hillside shagged with goldenrod and asters.
Gone, the fat groundhog humping through
a field of cornflowers, blue splendor
of weeds. Gone, the slopes of larch and maple
scattering down their gold and copper flakes,
their flecks of rust, across the sinking valley.

Now the hard time. Now the snow.
Now the black sticks, these thin shadows
of the ghosts they try to conjure back.

In the Beginning, There Was

Light was gathered, then was split into
the disparate balls that later were given names
and made to shine above the living stew
of water, protein, DNA and flames.
Animals were spawned, lain and calved.
Eventually, there resulted Man,
who, in his selfish loneliness, was halved,
and from that seed of bone an also-ran
called Woman was bred. She was made to ache
for anything the Man would have denied,
and so a fruit more sweet than wedding cake
was plucked and eaten. They were terrified.
They might have felt, when fallen from that place,
an absence of some agency, or grace.

PAWNING MY WEDDING RINGS

A tiny stone, two simple rings of gold
clinked upon the dull appraiser's tray.
"To honor, love and cherish, to have and to hold"—

or something like that, we were sternly told.
Ten years later, almost to the day,
this little stone, these rings of whitened gold

have lost all sentiment. Cash in the billfold,
money toward the mortgage, bills to pay,
if not to honor, love, have and hold.

Across the room, a guy barely old
enough to buy a beer scans the display
for a modest stone, a pretty ring of gold.

Such gleam and color, sparkles manifold!
A final glimpse as my rings are put away,
no longer mine to wear, to have and to hold.

I wish them well. I hope they'll be resold
to one whose heart won't wander, who won't betray
that faithful stone, those honest rings of gold;
who'll honor, love and cherish, who'll have and hold.

No Song

Again the lilacs bloom, the hillsides turn
a tender golden-green, woodpeckers

send out their firmly worded telegrams.
The greater part of our reflexive joy

is sheer relief—that winter has an end,
that spring returns, the world has not died

forever. The little lake is mirror-still,
a goose adrift in its false blue sky.

We prefer to think of beauty now,
banal and commonplace as it is—

as much as horror, which even sunstruck days,
such as this, assuredly contain.

A Summons

You start from sleep and run, your blue jeans still
unzipped, to answer the pounding at your door,
thinking *fire, rape, someone killed.*
You shout "Who's there?" and wait a beat before,
because you're human, you open anyway.
A gray, tumescent morning, large with rain,
and from the east, the soft unfurling day.
Your door upon the vast, unpeopled plain.
No sirens, no emergency.
Not even footprints coalesce the dew.
How could it be a dream, that urgency,
the certainty that someone needed you?
Your heart tattoos; your question steams the air.
You face the sun. *Who's there? Who's there? Who's there?*

Fortune Cookie Ghazal

Our hopes and expectations may not be
fulfilled by our reality, in bed.

The nectar of life is sweetest sipped from scores
of blooms, as sips the honeybee, in bed.

Be as a silk kimono: strong enough
to bind, yet softly flowing free, in bed.

Beware ambition! Those who reach too high
may fall upon their bended knee, in bed.

A single cherry blossom or a wooden toy
is often the best company, in bed.

Help! I'm trapped in a Chinese fortune cookie
factory! Please rescue me— in bed!

METAPHORLAND

We spend a lot of time there, my students and I.
We stroll through groves of oaks, dogwoods, cherries
in full-tilt blossom. We rank the sun,
from glist'ning chariot to baleful eye.
Like farmers, we argue over what the clouds
portend. We scan the sky for pigeons and hawks.

In town, we linger at lonely park benches,
empty bus stops, florists' window displays.
There are so many churches. So many schools.
We walk down darkened roads, winding roads,
forgotten roads, trafficked city roads,
dirt roads, and yes, some roads have been
more or less traveled than other roads.
All of them, it seems, are lined with graveyards.

At home, my students gaze out their windows
at sunsets, snow, rain, or playing children
who remind them of their younger selves.
I try to make my dinner. Not oysters.
Not a peach. Not madelines—food
content to be itself, a taco that's just
a taco. But oh, the olives! Oh, the red
and juicy heart of the tomato! And the onions,
dammit—the onions always make me cry.

THE MALE OF THE SPECIES

They flock to me, these pretty boys, with song
and showy summer jackets of black and gold.
They preen around the feeder, dive headlong.
They flock to me, these pretty boys. Their song
cries *look at me, look at me.* They throng
until the seed is spent. I'm getting old.
They flock to me, these pretty boys, with song
and thin, showy jackets of black and gold.

First House

The work— taping over baseboards and trim,
dabbing spackle, rolling paint I chose
both for its scrumptious name, Glazed Pecan,
and for its gold, glowing tone I hope
will keep me warm next winter—all of this
while sipping a beer and listening yet again
to Jeremy Irons drawling out *Lolita*—
this is pleasure born of selfishness.

Yet it's no less joyful, no less mine,
when solitude is broken. Danny, my friend,
drives up to show the new neighbor's house
to his kids, and out they tumble: Kevin, six,
and Leah, three: perfect blue-eyed cherubs
straight from Raphael or a greeting card.

When Kevin sees the backyard and its trees,
spruces and the just-leafing species
I can't yet identify, he asks
for a game of hide-and-seek-tag. I'm It,
he says. Okay. My count is loud and slow,
and when I turn, Danny's laughing, crouched
behind a bush, and Leah simply stands
in a drainage ditch, watching all the fun,
looking, really, inexcusably cute.
I found you! Tag! A soft tap on her arm.
Danny pops up, we chase, I tag,

he joins us in the search for Kev, who's tucked
himself beneath a willow. And when he runs,
we run—really run, full out, so fast
I lose a sandal in the tall grass
and go back, laughing. Anyone
who saw us would think we were a family.

It's not what I have chosen. It isn't mine.
But the sun casts bars of shade that we burst through,
and I am happy to have borrowed it:
this chasing after joy, this reaching out
to touch their hair, calling, *I found you, you're It.*

LATE BLIGHT

Mornings in late May, dew ascends
in smoky plumes from sunstruck roofs, while I
bend low, my hands deep in fresh-tilled earth.
Wrinkled beet seeds nestle in rows beside
the garlic and spring onions' tender spears.
The last of fall's potatoes have gone crazy
in basement isolation, shooting out
identically pale roots and stems.
I cut them into soft, bristly chunks
and bury them in furrows mulched with hay.
I leave plenty of room for kale and chard,
nudge the climbing peas toward the fence.
Tomato seedlings, toughening against
a late frost, bask in greenhouse sun.
I straighten, arch, pull against the ache.
Warmth, light, calls of chickadees
around the feeder, smells of earth and grass—
mornings such as this are reason enough
to go on living. Tonight I'll have to cut
my fingernails to rid them of the dirt.

Then, one day in August, a single Roma
overloaded with green fruit wilts
as if it alone were kissed by early frost.
Then all the Romas turn limp and spotted brown.
Then the cherries. Heirlooms. Early Girls.
And all my plants must be uprooted, bagged,

denied even the humble dignity

of compost, hauled away with the rest of the trash.

I gather up the fallen, blighted fruit

so there may be no seed of return.

And I was not wrong before: these small

earthly pleasures are all that we are offered.

And they shall ever come to such an end.

SUICIDE

A study by psychologist James Kaufman has concluded that poets—particularly female poets— are more likely than fiction writers, nonfiction writers and playwrights to have signs of mental illness, such as suicide attempts. He has dubbed this the "Sylvia Plath effect."

Such a lovely word we mustn't use.

Already, friends are keeping an eye on us.

They call on weekends, or when they haven't heard

from us in a while, just to check in.

Our co-workers are wary. If we crack

a few too many Plath jokes, we find ourselves

in mandatory counseling. And Mom,

who never trusted poetry, sighs

and sets another roll upon our plates.

We'd like to ask each other, take a poll:

How often do you think about it? Weekly?

Every day? Every fulsome night?

We want to find out what's normal, but

we know we're not the right ones to ask.

Studies blame the solipsistic "I"—

too much introspection fucks us up.

I disagree. If poets are in love

with language, then how could we not be seduced

by *suicide*, those silky vowel glides,

the sideways glance, all sibilance and curves?

It makes me think of a slinky red dress.

That color has always looked good on me.

CUTTERS

Some girls
        fall in love with scissors.
Some girls
        whisper secrets to
a sweet little paring knife
filched
        from their mother's kitchen drawer.

Some girls
        keep a razor blade
in their tidy billfolds, tucked among
their ticket stubs
        and mad money.

They wear long sleeves and knee-length skirts.
They keep the doors to their bedrooms closed.

The bright edge, the clean release,
the crimson kiss
        that stays with them,
reminds them with a pang each time
they bend or cross their legs
        that they
are loved—
        how can the girls say no?
Some girls
        don't know when to stop.

SCENE III

She floats along the silver stream,
A mermaid drifting in her sleep.
Her eyes are open, though adream,
Floating down the abettor stream.
The fish that peck her lips may seem
Like lovers. The coming days will sweep
Her cleanly down the bridgeless stream,
A mermaid drifting in her sleep.

If I Had a Nickel for Every Time

the deer in shabby winter coats, ribs
like tentpoles, nuzzled and licked clean the tube
of black oil seeds meant for chickadees—

the copper flash of maples in the wind
made me honestly believe that no one
had seen or loved maples like this before—

the ancient calico shit on the floor
and I forgave her, in her purrs and fluff,
and the damn cat just shit on the floor again—

the paperboy missed the porch, the mailman left
the box ajar in the rain, I cried in the car,
a starling brained itself on the window glass—

I showed up late, barged inside the church
through the wrong door, ate the last slice,
mocked the kids, insulted the host's new wife—

I made that same mistake—that handsome man
who hated women, that clever man who loved
public places and my ardent mouth—

I made a joke that turned into a knife,
flinched at a touch from one who had the right,
didn't understand, said nothing, nothing—

90

O I would drink those hard-won nickels down,
I'd weep and shed and gather up those coins,
I'd spend all love, all bitterness, again.

LARKIN AND WIFE

A soft-boiled egg, rye toast with jam
and soy links: the day's first compromise.
Philip steeps his tea, while my French press
takes the plunge. He blinks owlishly
against the morning sun, pats my ass,
and we bear our cups to separate offices.

They say writers shouldn't wed—at least,
not with other writers. And yet, they do,
and no one is surprised when soon the rumors
of drink and lovers fly, something breaks,
and indignant manuscripts go off to press.
My history, and Philip's chronic dread.

We like to think we've learned from our own fears,
and so we chart our course of days in love
and watchfulness, giving quarter here
or there, drawing gracious boundaries,
taking care to build what battlements
we need as hollow, false-fronted things.

Philip's porn, for instance. The magazines
stay nestled in his well-loved drawer, and I
pretend the unfamiliar muse is just
my great galumphing creature's fancy. A bit
of bondage, a spot of spanking— it's only play,
no real pain. The safeword is "Ted Hughes."

And in return, he suffers my movies, my cats,
my vegetarian diet. They give him matter
for complaint, and that makes him happy.
Music is hard; I tolerate his jazz,
have learned to like Bechet; he endures
my Dylan; at Wilco, kills his hearing aid.

It's hard. Of course it's hard. Isn't he
the poet of deprivation, death and gloom,
more than half in love with misery?
Aren't I my own unique disaster?
But doesn't being with him create for me
the contrasting, alien role of optimist?

Taps of slippered feet on floorboards, sighs
of books easing from shelves—these float to me
from down the hall, and I have learned to hear
in them not the tumblers of a lock
but domesticity's quiet hum,
like surf upon a rocky western shore.

A woman, like a man, is guardian
of her own happiness. Yet when at night
his weight like ballast shifts our mattress down,
even though he frets or snores—yet there
is my companion on the long, black ship.
There is love, my fellow passenger.

Notes

The epigraph by Emily Dickinson is taken from her poem 260 ["I'm Nobody! Who are You?"].

The epigraph by Neko Case is taken from her song "Hold On, Hold On" from *Fox Confessor Brings the Flood*.

"Helen of Sparta" was inspired by both Homer's *Odyssey* and Richard Howard's marvelous poem "Telemachus."

"From the Diary of Adèle Varens" takes its speaker and characters from the Charlotte Brontë novel *Jane Eyre*.

"Nancy Drew, 45, Posts on Match.com" takes its speaker from the Nancy Drew Mystery series of novels for young adults by Carolyn Keene.

"The Time Machine" takes its epigraph and inspiration from the novel *The Time Machine* by H.G. Wells.

Each of the poems in Section II, Box Set, is titled after and inspired by a film directed by Alfred Hitchcock.

The title of "'Winter comes to rule the varied year'" is taken from "The Seasons: Winter" by James Thomson.

Details of the life of Philip Larkin in "Larkin and Wife" are taken from *Philip Larkin: A Writer's Life* by Andrew Motion.

Acknowledgements

The author would like to acknowledge the following journals in which poems have previously appeared, sometimes in slightly different form.

Backwards City Review: "Portrait of My Mother as the Rush Hour Traffic Report" and "Portrait of My Sister as a Marble Ashtray"

Birmingham Poetry Review: "If I Had a Nickel for Every Time," "Pawning My Wedding Rings," "*Rear Window*" and "*North by Northwest*"

Iron Horse Literary Review: "Metaphorland"

The Louisville Review: "Aubade"

Measure: "Portrait of My Father as the Corner Bar" and "Ghost Story"

New South: "Phone Sex" and "From the Diary of Adèle Varens"

River Styx: "First House"

Southern Humanities Review: "Helen of Sparta," "*Rope*," "*Suspicion*," "Forest Creatures Prepare the Fairy Bride," "A Summons" and "Cutters"

Stone Canoe: "*The Birds*," "Nancy Drew, 45, Posts on Match.com," "Two Scenes" and "Scene III" (as "Three Scenes")

The Tampa Review: "Suicide"

32 Poems: "*Psycho*" and "Fortune Cookie Ghazal"

Unsplendid: "'Winter comes to rule the varied year'" and "The Housesitter's Note"

The author would also like to acknowledge Neko Case's fantastic album *Fox Confessor Brings the Flood*, under the influence of which many of these poems were written.

Author's Acknowledgements

Many thanks are due to many people for their help, both direct and indirect, with these poems. So here goes:

I am grateful to my friends and colleagues at Alfred University, especially Susan Morehouse, Allen Grove and David DeGraff, for their support. Thanks to Paul Strong for inspiring "If I Had a Nickel for Every Time." Thanks to Rob Reginio for introducing me to the music of Neko Case.

Thanks for twelve years of listening to me read at the Sewanee Writers' Conference, and for twelve years of mighty hugs and good feedback: Wyatt Prunty, Cheri Peters, Alan Shapiro, Charles Martin, Mary Jo Salter, Mark Jarman, Claudia Emerson, Danny Anderson, Mark Strand, Dan O'Brien, Margot Livesey, Randall Kenan, Claire Messud, Tony Earley, John Casey, Jill McCorkle, and the rest of the usual suspects.

Many thanks to the West Chester Poetry Conference crew: Michael Peich, Sam Gwynn, David Yezzi, Chelsea Rathburn, and many others.

Special thanks to Mike Levine and Erica Dawson for reading an early draft of this manuscript, and for their invaluable suggestions.

Thanks, Mom and Dad, for letting me be a poet.

Andrew Hudgins and Erin McGraw are pretty much the most amazing people on the planet. I just want everyone to know that.

Finally, thanks to my comrades in arms and best friends, the past and present staff of the Sewanee Writers' Conference. WCs, I need some help with these supplies. And a little piece of copper wire.

About the Author

Juliana Gray's first book of poetry, *The Man Under My Skin*, was published by River City Publishing in 2005. Her poems have appeared in *The Hopkins Review, New South, 32 Poems*, and elsewhere. A native of Alabama, she is an associate professor of English at Alfred University in western New York.

www.ingramcontent.com/pod-product-compliance
Lightning Source LLC
Chambersburg PA
CBHW021508090426
42739CB00007B/528